P9-DCD-614

FREE PUBLIC LIBRARY
UXBRIDGE MA 01569

World book
16.50

Persians

and Other Long-haired Cats

Editorial:
Editor in Chief: Paul A. Kobasa
Project Manager: Cassie Mayer
Writer: Karen Ingebretsen
Researcher: Cheryl Graham
Manager, Contracts & Compliance
 (Rights & Permissions): Loranne K. Shields
Indexer: David Pofelski

**Manufacturing/Production/
Graphics and Design:**
Director: Carma Fazio
Manufacturing Manager:
 Steven K. Hueppchen
Production/Technology Manager:
 Anne Fritzinger
Manager, Graphics and Design:
 Tom Evans
Coordinator, Design Development
 and Production:
 Brenda B. Tropinski
Senior Designer: Isaiah Sheppard
Photographs Editor: Kathy Creech
Cartographer: John Rejba

J
636.8

April 2015

For information about other World Book publications, visit our website at http://www.worldbookonline.com or call 1-800-WORLDBK (967-5325).

For information about sales to schools and libraries, call 1-800-975-3250 (United States), or 1-800-837-5365 (Canada).

© 2010 World Book, Inc. All rights reserved. This volume may not be reproduced in whole or in part in any form without prior written permission from the publisher.

WORLD BOOK and the GLOBE DEVICE are registered trademarks or trademarks of World Book, Inc.

World Book, Inc.
233 N. Michigan Avenue
Chicago, IL 60601
U.S.A.

Library of Congress Cataloging-in-Publication Data
Persians and other long-haired cats.
 p. cm. — (World Book's animals of the world)
 Includes index.
 Summary: "An introduction to Persians and other long-haired cats, presented in a highly illustrated, question-and-answer format. Features include fun facts, glossary, resource list, index, and scientific classification list"--Provided by publisher.
 ISBN 978-0-7166-1375-6
 1. Persian cat--Juvenile literature. 2. Longhair cats--Juvenile literature. I. World Book, Inc.
 SF449.P4P48 2010
 636.8'32--dc22
                    2009024284

World Book's Animals of the World
Set 6: ISBN: 978-0-7166-1365-7
Printed in China by Leo Paper Products LTD., Heshan, Guangdong
2nd printing August 2011

Picture Acknowledgments: Cover: © Dave King, Dorling Kindersley; © Robert W. Ginn, Alamy Images; © Dave King, Dorling Kindersley; © Linn Currie, Shutterstock; © Adisa, Shutterstock.

© David Askham, Alamy Images 23; © Robert W. Ginn, Alamy Images 35; © Juniors Bildarchiv/Alamy Images 31, 43; © Anthony Reynolds, Sylvia Cordaiy Photo Library/Alamy Images 17; © Petra Wegner, Alamy Images 33, 47; © Eric Kayne, Houston Chronicle/AP Images 55; © John Daniels, Ardea London 4, 29; © Dave King, Dorling Kindersley 7, 13; © Dorling Kindersley 25, 27; © Dreamstime 3, 19, 51, 57; © Purestock/Getty Images 61; © istockphoto 59; © Marcus Fuehrer, DPA/Landov 5, 49; © P. Wegner, Peter Arnold, Inc. 53; © Shutterstock 5, 37, 39, 41, 45; © Photononstop/SuperStock 21; © Jerry Shulman, SuperStock 15.

Illustrations: WORLD BOOK illustration by Roberta Polfus 9.

World Book's Animals of the World

Persians
and Other Long-haired Cats

WORLD
BOOK

a Scott Fetzer company
Chicago
www.worldbookonline.com

Contents

What Is a Long-haired Cat?

All cats are members of the family Felidae *(FEE luh dy)*. This family includes the lion, tiger, panther, and leopard. It also includes domestic cats. Domestic cats are smaller members of the cat family that were tamed by human beings long ago and which are now often kept as pets. Whether small or large, all cats are carnivores *(KAHR nuh vawrs),* or meat eaters, and they are skillful hunters. In addition, all cats are warm-blooded and are mammals—animals that feed their young with milk made by the mother.

Long-haired cats are domestic cats that have long fur instead of short fur. A long-haired cat may have a single or double coat. The coat can be anywhere between 2 and 6 inches (5 and 15 centimeters) long.

Persian cats are known for their long, fine-textured, glossy coats. Their fur stands out from the body and forms a large ruff and a full, brushlike tail. Persians should be indoor-only cats because their fur is easily matted.

6

A Persian cat

What Does a Persian Cat Look Like?

Persians are elegant cats known for their round features. They have a broad, short body and short, strong legs. Like all cats, Persians have strong jaws and sharp teeth that are especially well suited for hunting. However, their faces are rounder than those of most other cats. They have short, snub noses and short necks. Their large, round eyes are set wide apart. Most Persians have copper eyes.

Persians and most other cats have five toes on each front paw. Each toe ends in a sharp, hooklike claw. The claws are usually retracted (held back) under the skin. Several spongy pads of thick skin cover the bottoms of a cat's feet.

A Persian's body is covered in long, thick fur that needs daily grooming. If you're not willing to commit to this routine, a Persian is not the right cat for you. Also keep in mind that Persians shed a lot. You will need to plan on vacuuming or sweeping often, or you'll end up wearing some of that gorgeous cat hair, too!

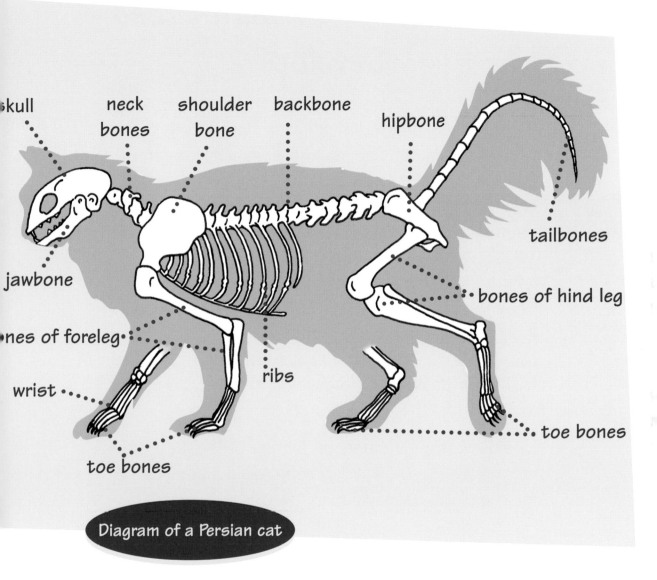

skull

neck bones

shoulder bone

backbone

hipbone

jawbone

tailbones

bones of foreleg

bones of hind leg

wrist

ribs

toe bones

toe bones

Diagram of a Persian cat

9

How Did the Persian Breed Develop?

A breed is a group of animals that has the same type of ancestors. No one knows exactly how the Persian breed of cats developed. Long-haired cats lived in the Middle East for several thousand years, but they probably did not appear in Europe until the 1500's. At that time, European traders brought home long-haired cats from Persia (now Iran) and Turkey. These cats were mated with European breeds, and their offspring (young) became the breed we now call Persians. Persian cats have been carefully bred for hundreds of years to develop the look they have today.

The Persian is the most popular of the 40 breeds recognized by the Cat Fanciers' Association (CFA), the major cat association in the United States.

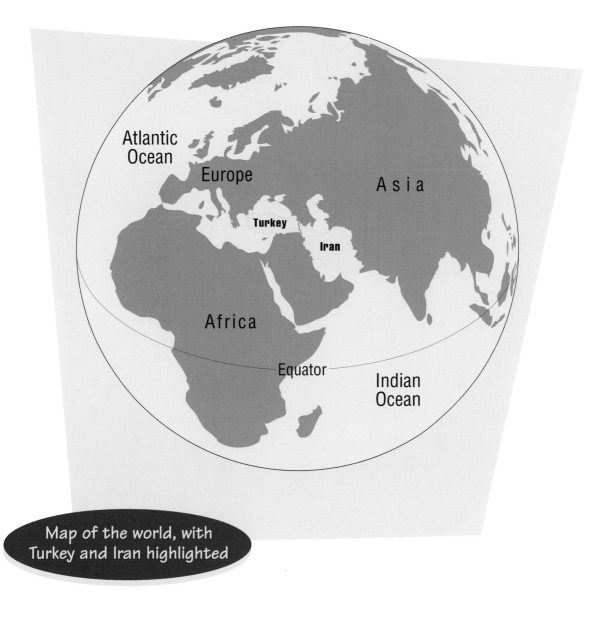

Atlantic
Ocean

Europe

A s i a

Turkey

Iran

Africa

Equator

Indian
Ocean

Map of the world, with
Turkey and Iran highlighted

11

What Colors Do Persian Cats Come In?

Persian cats come in so many colors and patterns that it would almost be easier to list those they don't come in!

Solid-color Persians can be black, white, blue, red, cream, lilac, or chocolate. (In Persian cats, "blue" is actually gray, "red" is actually orange, and "lilac" is lavender with pinkish tones.) Persians with two or more colors may be a combination of any of these colors. They have different names depending on the pattern of the colors. A few of these are tabby, tortoiseshell, and calico.

There are also Persians with "tipped" coats, where the tip of each hair is a different color than the base. And Himalayans, which developed by crossing Persians with Siamese, have the distinctive "points" (areas of darker color) that Siamese cats are known for.

12

Persians come in many different colors.

What Kind of Personality Might a Persian Cat Have?

Persians are gentle, sweet cats. They are best suited for an indoor "life of leisure" and are content to nap in the sun or lounge near their owners. They are quiet, laid-back, and not as vocal as some other breeds. Many seem to enjoy "posing" in the home as if they were precious collectibles. They are affectionate cats that need attention from their owners.

Most Persian cats are good with children and can get along with other household pets if they are properly introduced. They do not do well when left alone for long periods. A lack of attention can cause a Persian cat to become nervous, shy, or aggressive. Some owners get a second cat to keep their Persian company.

The Persian cat's calm personality makes it a good choice for a family pet. And its beautiful appearance is hard to resist.

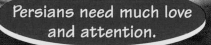

Persians need much love
and attention.

What Should You Look for When Choosing a Persian Kitten?

When choosing a Persian kitten, look for one that is healthy. Some signs of good health are: alertness; a sturdy body; quiet breathing (no wheezing, coughing, or sneezing); bright, clear eyes; a clean, slightly moist nose; firm, pink gums with no sores; no lumps or bumps on the body; and a glossy coat with no bald patches. Healthy kittens should also be active, and spend much of their time playing and fighting with their littermates.

To test a kitten's hearing, have someone come up behind it and clap his or her hands. The kitten should be startled by this sudden sound and look toward the source. To test eyesight, see if the kitten will play with a small toy placed in front of it.

A kitten should not be taken from its mother until it is fully weaned (accustomed to food other than its mother's milk). This usually occurs between 2 and 3 months of age.

Persian kittens

17

Should You Get an Older Persian Instead of a Kitten?

Kittens are very active and may be more work than you're prepared to handle, so you may want to adopt an older Persian cat. There are many advantages to this. An older Persian cat is likely to be calmer. And, an older cat may have already had an operation to prevent it from producing young. It may also have been tested for infectious diseases and is often already used to living with people. In addition, you will be able to see what its personality is like.

Animal shelters in your area may well have Persians available for adoption. Rescue groups help to find new homes for purebred cats, including Persians. Or, breeders may sometimes have Persians that are being retired from the show ring that are ready for a loving new home.

Older cats tend to be
less active than kittens.

19

What Does a Persian Cat Eat?

Most Persian cats eat a diet of commercial cat food, which can either be canned or dry. Both types of food are good for a cat. Canned food usually contains more meat, while dry food helps to clean a cat's teeth. For that reason, many owners offer canned food once or twice daily and leave dry food out at all times so the cat can "snack" when it chooses. It is a good idea to change the flavors often. Otherwise, your cat may become so used to eating only one flavor that it refuses everything else.

Persians also need to eat grass occasionally. This helps them to cough up hairballs, which they get from licking their thick fur. Pet stores sell grass seed kits for growing your own, or flats with grass already growing in them.

Make sure your Persian has fresh drinking water at all times.

A Persian cat eating

Where Should a Persian Cat Sleep?

A Persian cat should have its own place to sleep. Pet stores and companies online sell cat beds in every style imaginable. Whatever bed you purchase, clean it often so it does not become a home for fleas.

Cats spend much time sleeping, and chances are your Persian won't always sleep in its bed. It may choose to cat-nap on your bed or the back of the sofa. Your favorite chair may become its favorite chair, too. Your cat may think a laundry basket is the perfect place for a snooze, especially if it's filled with nice, soft clothes. Even an in-box on a desk can be a good bed if you're studying nearby and available for petting duty!

Many cats choose to rest in warm, comfortable spaces—often near heating vents. Persians especially like to perch on a sunny windowsill or cuddle in bed, under the covers with their owner.

Cats love to sleep in cozy places.

How Do You Groom a Persian Cat?

You must comb and brush your Persian cat's fur every day. This is absolutely necessary to prevent the cat's fur from getting tangled and matted. It also helps to prevent the cat from getting hairballs. And it helps collect the hair your cat sheds. Moving from head to tail, comb all of your cat's fur first with a wide-toothed metal comb, then repeat with a fine-toothed metal comb. (Avoid nylon combs, because they create static electricity.) If you find any matted fur, get an adult's help in handling it. After combing, brush the cat's fur with a natural-bristle brush.

Persian cats' eyes water more than those of most breeds and develop a sticky substance that stains. Have an adult help you gently wipe the lower lids with a damp, soap-free washcloth. (Do not rub the eyeball directly.) If needed, ask your veterinarian about products to treat eye stains.

A veterinarian or other adult should trim a Persian cat's nails regularly. An adult should also clean the cat's ears using a cotton ball or cotton swab.

24

Grooming a Persian cat

Should You Give Your Persian Cat a Bath?

Persian cats need to be bathed at least once a month. Dry shampoos, which are available at pet stores, are helpful for keeping a Persian clean, but a wet bath is preferred.

Unfortunately, most cats hate to get wet, so two adults should perform the task of bathing. They should trim your cat's nails before bathing to reduce scratching.

A cat should be washed in a washbasin or bathtub with lukewarm water. Place a towel or rubber mat at the bottom of the basin or tub to prevent your cat from slipping. One person should hold the cat still, keeping a firm hold of its legs and mouth, while the other person bathes the cat.

Use a shampoo especially for cats. Make sure to keep the shampoo out of the cat's ears, eyes, nose, and mouth. Rinse the cat well, so no soap remains. After the bath, dry the cat thoroughly. Wrap it in a towel and gently pat it dry (do not rub).

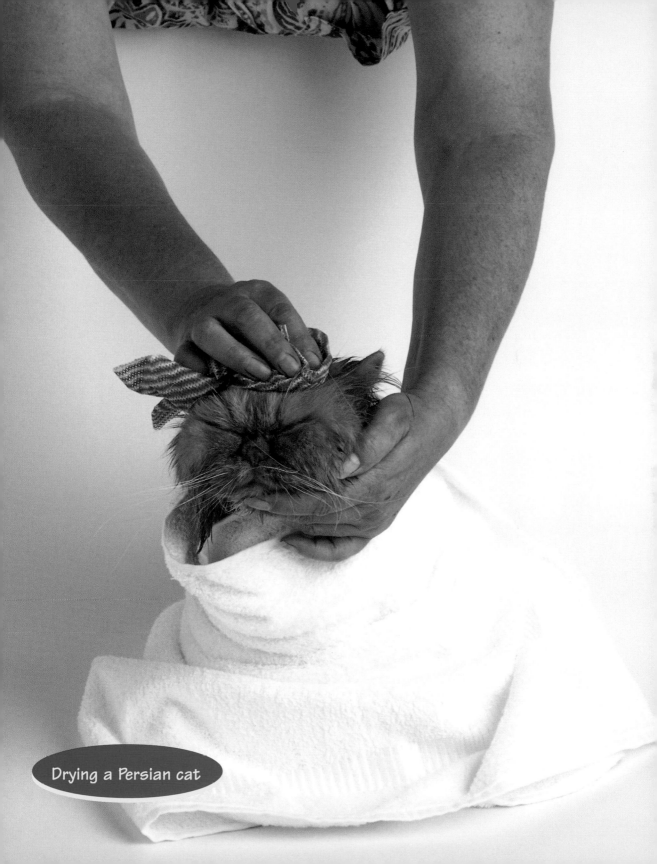

Drying a Persian cat

What Kinds of Training Are Needed?

All indoor cats need certain kinds of training to make them good housemates. If you have a kitten, begin training when it is about 5 weeks old.

Cats should be trained to claw a scratching post instead of carpeting, draperies, and furniture. A bark-covered log or a piece of wood covered with carpeting, rope, or coarse fabric makes a good scratching post. Rub some catnip, a strongly scented herb that many cats love to sniff, into the post to attract the cat's interest. Guide the cat's front paws down the post. Whenever the cat begins to claw another object, correct the animal immediately and take it to the post. To correct your cat, do not scold or hit it, but gently squirt some water on it.

Many cats like to perch wherever they please, including kitchen counters and dinner tables—places that must be kept free of animal hair and germs. To train your cat that these places are off limits, you must pick up and remove the cat immediately after it jumps onto the surface.

28

Clawing a scratching post

What Kinds of Exercise or Play Are Needed?

Most Persian cats are kept indoors. Even an indoor-only cat can get all the exercise it needs. Your Persian can learn to fetch a crumpled ball of paper. It will probably also like playing with a tennis ball or table tennis ball, or batting at a toy dangling from a string or flexible wire. Your cat will try to pounce on a toy that's pulled along on a string.

If you do want your cat to enjoy the outdoors, and if you're patient, you may be able to teach it to walk on a leash. If your cat enjoys this, you can make it a regular part of your routine. If not, don't worry—your cat can get plenty of exercise indoors.

30

Persian kittens are especially playful.

Should You Breed Your Persian Cat?

Each year, millions of unwanted cats are abandoned, and many of these cats end up in animal shelters. Because the problem of unwanted cats is so serious, owners should not allow their cats to have kittens unless a good home can be provided for them.

A veterinarian can perform an operation to prevent cats from being able to reproduce (make more of themselves). The operation is called neutering. When performed on a female cat, it is commonly called spaying. This operation can be performed any time after 6 weeks of age.

If you have a female cat that becomes pregnant (expecting young), talk to your veterinarian about what to feed the mother while she is pregnant and also when she is feeding her young.

A Persian cat and her litter

What Are Other Kinds of Long-haired Cats?

The Cat Fanciers' Association recognizes 12 breeds of long-haired cats, including the Persian. Other cat associations recognize different long-haired breeds. Canada has the Canadian Cat Association; the United Kingdom has the Governing Council of the Cat Fancy; and Australia has the Co-ordinating Cat Council of Australia.

Some breeds include both long- and short-haired types. The Selkirk rex is a large cat that comes in two coat lengths, short and long. These curly-haired cats even have curly whiskers!

There are also short- and long-haired varieties of the Scottish fold. Many of these cats have ears that fold toward the face and downward. The unusual ears, combined with the cats' round faces, give them an owlish look.

The domestic longhair, also known as the American longhair, is a non-pedigreed breed of long-haired cat.

34

A Selkirk rex

What Is a Somali Cat?

A Somali cat is an active, intelligent cat. It has earned the nickname "little fox" because of its large ears, bushy tail, full ruff (fine hairs around the cat's neck), and masked face (dark-rimmed eyes with lighter fur surrounding them).

The Somali breed developed from the offspring (young) of Abyssinian cats, a short-haired breed. The Somali looks like the Abyssinian except for its soft, medium-length double coat, which has blue, reddish, or brown bands.

Somali cats love to play. They have energy bursts several times a day. At those times they will zip around, chasing balls and leaping into the air. They will run sideways, like a monkey does. These cats can even turn on faucets and open cupboards!

A Somali cat

37

What Is a Himalayan Cat?

That depends on whom you ask! Some associations that register pedigreed breeds consider the Himalayan cat a type of Persian cat. Others consider it a separate breed. The Cat Fanciers' Association, which divides Persians into seven color divisions for purposes of competition, considers the Himalayan a Persian.

The Himalayan has the same color pattern as a Siamese cat. It has a solid color over the trunk of the body and a contrasting color on the face, ears, feet, and tail. It's not surprising that the Himalayan looks like a long-haired version of the Siamese, because it developed as a cross between the Siamese and the Persian.

This cat is named for the Himalayan rabbit, whose fur has a similar contrasting color pattern.

A Himalayan cat

What Is a Maine Coon Cat?

A Maine coon cat is one of the largest breeds of domestic cats. It has a broad, muscular body. Its markings are similar to those of a raccoon, which may be where the "coon" part of its name came from.

The breed developed in New England during the 1800's. Its ancestors probably included both American short-haired cats and long-haired cats brought to Maine by sailors. The cat's heavy, silky coat helped to keep it warm during the long New England winters. Its large, round paws made it well suited for running across snow.

Today, Maine coon cats are popular family pets. They get along well with children and dogs, and they have easygoing personalities. They are well known for the chirps and trills they use to "talk" with human beings.

A Maine coon cat

What Is a Siberian Cat?

A Siberian cat is a very large, semi-long-haired cat that has a rich, full coat in winter and a somewhat shorter coat in summer. The Siberian is the national cat of Russia and is named for Siberia, a large region of Russia with extreme, cold weather about half the year.

The Siberian is an ancient breed, dating back possibly as far as 1,000 years. Though these cats are common in Russia, they are extremely rare in the United States. The first Siberians were introduced to the United States in 1990. Since then, their numbers have grown slowly but steadily.

Siberians are loyal pets; many greet their owners at the door and follow them around the house. Like Maine coons, they converse in chirps and trills.

A Siberian cat

What Is a Norwegian Forest Cat?

A Norwegian forest cat is an ancient breed that is mentioned in Norwegian mythology. It is a large, muscular cat with a triangular head and large ears with prominent tufts. Its thick fur has a woolly undercoat and a full, thick ruff like a miniature lion's mane.

Like Siberian cats, Norwegian forest cats shed some of their heavy "winter coat" when the warmer weather arrives. But their long tails (some as long as 12 inches, or 30 centimeters) stay full and fluffy the year around.

"Wegies" *(WEE-gees)*, as they are known, are energetic, playful cats. Though the Norwegian forest cat was originally an outdoor breed, living in forests and on farms, these cats do well as household pets.

44

A Norwegian forest cat

How Do Cats Communicate?

Though cats can't talk, they have many ways of communicating with other cats—and with people. Cats meow to say hello or to show that they are hungry, lonely, or curious about something. They use their larynx (voice box) in the throat to purr, which they do mostly when they're relaxed.

A cat's eyes and body language can also tell you how it's feeling. A happy cat often lies on its chest with its eyes half closed. If it's in a playful mood or in need of some belly rubbing, a cat may roll over on one side and wave a paw in the air.

Cats are not always in a playful mood. If a cat gives you a direct stare, extends its claws, and folds back its ears, it's saying, "Back off." Also, leave a cat alone if it flicks its tail from side to side, arches its back, or puffs up its fur. Other signs of an angry cat include hissing, growling, or even screaming.

An angry kitten

Why Do Cats Always Land on Their Feet?

A cat's physical traits and natural instincts help the animal to almost always land on its feet.

Cats have keen sense of balance, which allows them to easily walk along the tops of narrow fences or along narrow ledges. They also have sharp eyesight, which helps them to judge distances. And they have a "righting reflex"—that is, they will instinctively work to turn themselves upright the minute they leap into the air. When a cat falls, it whips the tail and twists its body to land on its feet.

A cat's flexible backbone helps to cushion the impact when it lands. When its feet hit the ground, a cat will arch its back to help absorb the impact.

Of course, cats can hurt themselves if they fall from high places, so be sure to keep your cat away from open windows or balconies.

Cats have a keen sense of balance.

How Can You Make Your Home Safe for a Cat?

Cats are very curious and love to explore, so keep all medicines and household cleaners locked away. Clean up all spills right away, and then rinse the floor with clear water.

Cats love to play with string, but they love to chew on it, too. This isn't good for them. Keep all string, yarn, ribbon, and thread out of your cat's reach. Tuck electrical cords out of the way—some cats like to chew on them.

Keep the clothes dryer door shut so your cat can't climb in unnoticed. Keep the toilet seat lid down. Make sure all windows have screens to prevent your cat from escaping.

Some houseplants, such as aloe, hydrangeas *(hy DRAYN juhs)*, lilies, and geraniums, are poisonous to cats. Check the Web site of the Cat Fanciers' Association (http://www.cfa.org/articles/plants.html) for a full list, or ask your veterinarian.

A Persian cat at home

What Basic Equipment Is Needed for a Cat?

The first thing you'll need is a carrier—something in which to place the new cat for its trip to your home, and later to take it to the vet. You will also need:

- Collar and I.D. tags—even an indoors-only cat needs these. You can't be sure your cat won't escape and, if it does, you need a way to show people who it belongs to.

- Litter box and litter—at least one box per cat

- Scratching post

- Bed

- Food and water bowls

- Grooming tools (brush and comb, nail clippers, toothbrush)

Pet stores sell all sorts of cat toys, but there are lots of homemade toys that your pet will love, too. You can find instructions for making cat toys on the Internet.

A cat carrier

What Is a Cat Show Like?

In most cat shows, the animals are judged on how well they conform to (match up with) the standards for that particular breed. Many different groups hold cat shows. Some shows are held by registries—groups that register particular breeds of cats. Many shows have a category in which mixed-breed, or household cats, can compete.

The Cat Fanciers' Association sponsors many cat shows in the United States and in some other countries. The group has a Junior Showmanship Program designed to help young people from ages 8 through 15 learn how to show a cat. In Junior Showmanship classes, exhibitors are not judged on the quality of the cat. Instead, the exhibitor is judged on his or her ability to handle the cat and on their knowledge of the breed.

According to the guidelines of the Cat Fanciers' Association, an ideal Persian cat should look sturdy, well balanced, and round with eyes that suggest a sweet temperament. Its coat should be long, shiny, and thick but have a fine texture.

A Persian cat at a
cat show

What Are Some Common Signs of Illness in Cats?

Any behavior that is not normal for your cat may be a sign that it is not feeling well. For instance, if your cat growls at you or bites you without reason, it may be unwell. When in doubt, your family should call the vet's office to discuss any concerns. Common signs of illness in cats include:

- Diarrhea or repeated vomiting. (All cats occasionally vomit, especially after eating grass, or to get rid of hairballs, but repeated vomiting is not normal.)

- Wheezing sounds or other breathing difficulty.

- A cat biting or scratching itself, especially if it has caused sores.

- A cat refusing food and/or water.

- A cat that is always hungry or thirsty.

- Frequent attempts to relieve itself.

- Sudden weight loss.

- Dull fur or shedding more fur than usual.

Observing your cat's behavior will help you spot signs of illness.

What Routine Veterinary Care Is Needed?

Routine visits to the vet will help your cat to stay healthy. Cats need immunizations (shots) against viruses, including rabies and the feline leukemia virus complex. Rabies is a deadly disease caused by a virus that destroys part of the brain. Feline leukemia is a form of cancer that affects the cat's blood-forming organs and other parts of the body.

Cats should have a checkup at least once a year. Older cats usually have checkups more often. If your cat is 10 years or older, ask your vet about this.

Parasites can be a problem for cats. Your Persian may develop internal parasites, such as roundworms or tapeworms. Or it may develop external ones, such as fleas or ticks. Your vet can diagnose and treat these conditions. Regular, monthly medication is often recommended to prevent heartworm infections, caused by a type of parasite.

All cats need regular medical checkups.

What Are Your Responsibilities as an Owner?

As an owner, it is your responsibility to make sure your cat gets routine veterinary care. You should also consult a vet any time your cat appears unwell. In addition, you should have your cat neutered.

You must feed your cat at regular times and make sure it always has fresh water. You should not leave your cat alone for long periods.

You must guard your cat's safety. If you do plan to let your cat outside, do so only in an enclosed area from which it cannot escape. Your cat needs a collar and I.D. tags, as well.

Finally, think carefully before you have a cat declawed. Many humane societies feel that the operation, even on just the front paws, is cruel and unnecessary, and it leaves a cat defenseless should it ever escape from its home.

Be sure to spend much time caring for your cat.

Long-haired Cat Fun Facts

→ The Maine coon cat is the official state cat of Maine.

→ The first major cat show in the United States was held in 1895. The winner was a Maine coon cat named Cosey.

→ Queen Victoria of the United Kingdom (1819-1901) owned two blue Persian cats.

→ In the United Kingdom, Persian cats are known as Longhairs and each color is considered a separate breed.

→ The ragdoll cat is born white and slowly develops its color and pattern over the next two years.

→ The Turkish van is well known for its fondness for swimming.

→ Snowbell the cat in the film version of *Stuart Little* (1999) is a white Persian.

→ Cats can run about 30 miles (48 kilometers) per hour.

→ Some experts estimate that a cat can make more than 60 different sounds, ranging from a soft purr to a loud wail.

→ A cat has more than a dozen muscles that control ear movement.

Glossary

ancestor An animal from which another animal is directly descended. Usually, *ancestor* is used to refer to an animal more removed than a parent or grandparent.

breed To produce animals by carefully selecting and mating them for certain traits. Also, a group of animals having the same type of ancestors.

domestic A tame animal living with or under the care of humans. Cats, dogs, and rabbits are some domestic animals.

groom To take care of an animal, for example, by combing, brushing, or trimming its coat.

hairball A pellet or mass of hair accumulated in an animal's stomach.

neuter To operate on a male animal to make it unable to produce young.

parasite An organism (living creature) that feeds on or in the body of another organism, often causing harm to the being on which it feeds.

pedigreed An animal with a document or certificate showing ancestors with unmixed breeding.

purebred An animal whose parents are known to have belonged to one breed.

ruff The longer, fringelike hairs around a cat's neck.

shed To throw off or lose hair, skin, fur, or other body covering.

spay To operate on a female animal to make it unable to have young.

tabby A brown, gray, or tawny cat with darker streaks and spots.

trait A feature or characteristic particular to an animal or breed of animals.

warm-blooded Having warm blood or blood that stays about the same temperature regardless of the air or water around the animal.

63

Index <small>(**Boldface** indicates a photo, map, or illustration.)</small>

For more information about Persians and other long-haired cats, try these resources:

Books:
Cats by Seymour Simon (HarperCollins, 2009)

Cats: 500 Questions Answered by David Sands (Hamlyn, 2005)

Essential Cat by Caroline Davis (Reader's Digest, 2005)

Everything Cat by Marty Crisp (NorthWord Press, 2003)

Persian Cats: A Complete Pet Owner's Manual by Ulrike Müller (Barron's, 2004)

Web sites:
Canadian Cat Association
http://www.cca-afc.com/

Cat Fanciers' Association
http://www.cfa.org/breeds/profiles/persian.html

Co-ordinating Cat Council of Australia
http://cccofa.asn.au

The Governing Council of the Cat Fancy (United Kingdom)
http://www.gccfcats.org/

Purebred Cat Breed Rescue
http://purebredcatbreedrescue.org/rescues.htm

Cat Classification

Scientists classify animals by placing them into groups. The animal kingdom is a group that contains all the world's animals. Phylum, class, order, and family are smaller groups. Each phylum contains many classes. A class contains orders, an order contains families, and a family contains genuses. One or more species belong to each genus. Here is how the animals in this book fit into this system.

Animals with backbones and their relatives (Phylum Chordata)
Mammals (Class Mammalia)
Carnivores (Order Carnivora)

Cats and their relatives (Family Felidae)

Domestic cat . . . . *Felis catus*